1001 WAYS TO
TRANQUILLITY

ARCTURUS

With special thanks to Paul Lucas

ARCTURUS

This edition published in 2012 by Arcturus Publishing Limited
26/27 Bickels Yard, 151–153 Bermondsey Street,
London SE1 3HA

ISBN: 978-1-84858-552-2
AD002249EN

Printed in China

Contents

Introduction

As our lives become increasingly hectic it's ever more important that we find refuges of tranquillity and relaxation. Yet often the more we seek tranquillity the harder it seems to find. The very act of searching can leave us even more frustrated and anxious than when we started.

This little book is designed to act as a guide to steer you towards your own garden of calm, whenever you need to find it. It will reassure

you that tranquillity can be found in the most unlikely places, and remind you that it is not where you look but how you see that determines whether you find your haven of peace. A mixture of inspirational quotes and practical tips will help you to relax and maintain your equilibrium, whether you're on your own or with others, at home or at work. Dip into its pages whenever life threatens to overwhelm you, and allow the calming voices within to transport you to the sanctuary of tranquillity which you carry within you at all times, no matter how far away it may sometimes appear to be.

What is Tranquillity?

How do we define tranquillity? How can we ever hope to find it unless we know what we are looking for?

In great moments life seems neither right nor wrong, but something greater: it seems inevitable.

Margaret Sherwood

Tranquillity can be found in the tiniest of moments, like when you take a single deep breath in the middle of a busy day.

Often just being around familiar things can make you feel calm.

Slow down and you might find that the dreams you thought you were chasing were actually trying to catch up with you.

Serenity is knowing that your worst shot is still pretty good. *Johnny Miller*

The ideal of calm exists in a sitting cat.
Jules Renard

Nature does not fear change and neither should you. Each new season is beautiful in its own way.

The first step to tranquillity is acceptance.

Tranquillity is being able to relax when you don't have time to.

Making things easier for yourself should never make you feel guilty.

Boredom is the feeling that everything is a waste of time; serenity, that nothing is.
Thomas Szasz

If you feel you are part of the world rather than separate from it, then you are becoming tranquil.

You will never find true tranquillity until you learn to love yourself.

Be positive and you will attract positive things.

When you find your inner equilibrium, work becomes almost effortless.

It's not so much how busy you are, but why you are busy. The bee is praised; the mosquito is swatted.

Marie O'Conner

Focus on your needs rather than your desires in order to find tranquillity.

Don't try and 'fit in'. Just try and be who you really are.

Tranquillity is an attitude rather than a destination.

All of the animals, excepting man, know that the principal business of life is to enjoy it.

Samuel Butler

Knowing that nothing lasts forever can produce a wonderful sense of calm.

Don't believe you are too busy to indulge yourself; even the briefest moments of relaxation can invigorate you for the rest of the day.

Anxiety is caused by thinking you should be someone else. Tranquillity comes when you relax and enjoy being yourself.

What is life but the angle of vision? A man is measured by the angle at which he looks at objects.

Ralph Waldo Emerson

Imagine a tranquil setting and you will immediately reduce your level of anxiety

You will find tranquillity when you truly feel you deserve it.

How blessed are some people, whose lives have no fears, no dreads, to whom sleep is a blessing that comes nightly, and brings nothing but sweet dreams.
Bram Stoker

Write down pleasant dreams so that you can revisit them when you are under stress.

It is often hard to feel truly tranquil when surrounded by material things.

Calm self-confidence is as far from conceit as the desire to earn a decent living is remote from greed.

Channing Pollock

If you don't open the doors of your mind now and then, stress will never be able to leave you.

Impatience is the enemy of tranquillity.

If only we'd stop trying to be happy we'd have a pretty good time.
Edith Wharton

Don't overlook the miraculous nature of seemingly ordinary things.

If you don't give yourself permission to be tranquil, how will you ever find peace?

When they are alone they want to be with others, and when they are with others they want to be alone. After all, human beings are like that. *Gertrude Stein*

There are neither yesterdays nor tomorrows, there is only here and now.

Remind yourself that to keep going is a type of victory.

There is no pleasure in having nothing to do; the fun is in having lots to do and not doing it.
Mary Wilson Little

Don't imagine that everyone else is more contented than you are.

Thinking positive is the first major step on the path to tranquillity.

Millions long for immortality who don't know what to do on a rainy afternoon. *Susan Ertz*

Take time off when you feel under the weather. Continuing to work will only lead to your health deteriorating.

Not taking risks can be as stressful as taking risks.

There are two rules in life: Rule #1: Don't sweat the small stuff. Rule #2: Everything is small stuff.

Finn Taylor

Take responsibility for your choices and you'll start to feel more in control of your life.

When you are unhappy, is there anything more maddening than to be told that you should be contented with your lot?
Kathleen Norris

Accepting that life is full of pressures is a key step to finding tranquillity.

Be happy whenever you have done your best, no matter what the result.

Better by far you should forget and smile than that you should remember and be sad.

Christina Rossetti

Sometimes you have to bite your tongue and just let things go.

Seeing things from other people's perspective helps to bring harmony into your life.

I don't own an inch of land, but all I see is mine.
Lucy Larcom

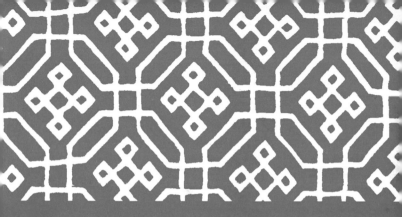

Don't be afraid to ask others for help.

Be curious: understanding leads, ultimately, to tranquillity.

If you realize too acutely how valuable time is, you are too paralysed to do anything.
Katharine Butler Hathaway

You will never find tranquillity by ignoring reality.

It doesn't matter what you believe as long as your life has meaning. If it doesn't, you will always feel anxious.

To achieve the impossible dream, try going to sleep. *Joan Klempner*

Don't be afraid to dream big.

Tranquillity is something you choose, not something that happens to you.

Fear cannot be banished, but it can be calm and without panic; it can be mitigated by reason and evaluation.

Vannevar Bush

Swim with the tide rather than against it whenever possible.

Make friends with your inner child and you'll never be far from tranquillity.

Half our life is spent trying to find something to do with the time we have rushed through life trying to save. *Will Rogers*

Confront your fears: they are what prevent you from finding tranquillity.

The secret to finding tranquillity lies in self-control.

There must be quite a few things that a hot bath won't cure, but I don't know many of them.
Sylvia Plath

We can never hope to understand anything completely: remind yourself that not knowing is okay.

Remind yourself of what really matters to you, and pursue only that. If you follow your heart then you will find tranquillity along the way.

There are two ways of meeting difficulties. You alter the difficulties or you alter yourself to meet them.
Phyllis Bottome

Let go of the past if you want to find peace in the future.

Selfishness is perhaps the biggest barrier to tranquillity.

I still miss those I loved who are no longer with me but I find I am grateful for having loved them. The gratitude has finally conquered the loss.

Rita Mae Brown

Let go of your anger or it will always poison your heart.

To find true tranquillity you need to be at peace not just with yourself but also with others, so strive to find the good in everyone you meet.

Weather means more when you have a garden. There's nothing like listening to a shower and thinking how it is soaking in around your green beans.

Marcelene Cox

Remind yourself that you are important, special and unique.

Work, look for peace and calm in work: you will find it nowhere else.
Dmitri Mendeleev

Leave the phone to ring now and then: you'll soon realize that if the call is important then the caller will phone back.

If you focus on doing something well you will often find tranquillity creeps up on you without you even realizing it.

Make the most of what you have rather than worrying about what you don't have.

To hear pure silence you have to listen hard.

There is more to life than increasing its speed.

Mohandas Gandhi

Tranquillity is whatever makes you feel most like yourself.

To find peace, give love.

While conscience is our friend, all is at peace; however once it is offended, farewell to a tranquil mind.

Mary Wortley Montagu

Tranquillity tends to descend upon those who remember to laugh at themselves.

If you carry tranquillity in your heart you can be at peace even amongst a bustling crowd.

You can't be everything to everybody, so concentrate on just being everything you can be to yourself.

True silence is the rest of the mind; it is to the spirit what sleep is to the body, nourishment and refreshment.

William Penn

Make sure you get plenty of sleep: nothing is more tranquil than a dream.

Even on the darkest days, life is full of little miracles. Learn to be grateful for them.

Gratitude changes the pangs of memory into a tranquil joy.

Dietrich Bonhoeffer

Don't over think things, or you will never be at peace.

Take a detour from the main road now and then: tranquillity lurks in the strangest nooks and crannies.

It is impossible to enjoy idling thoroughly unless one has plenty of work to do.
Jerome K. Jerome

Try and look at everything
as if you were viewing it for
the first time.

**Don't compare
yourself to
other people;
just be content
to be yourself.**

The greatest weapon against stress is our ability to choose one thought over another.
William James

The more you learn to like yourself the more you will enjoy spending time with yourself.

Trusting in others will bring you peace.

Sometimes just slowing down slightly is as relaxing as a rest.

There is no need to go to India or anywhere else to find peace. You will find that deep place of silence right in your room, your garden or even your bathtub.

Elisabeth Kübler-Ross

Do not worry unduly about financial matters. There is more to life than money.

If your expectations of yourself are too high, then you will always be disappointed in yourself.

Happiness is the harvest of a quiet eye.

Austin O'Malley

Tranquillity arrives in its own good time: don't try and hurry it along.

Learn to only concern yourself with things you can actually change.

Stress is an ignorant state. It believes that everything is an emergency.
Natalie Goldberg

All the tranquillity you crave is already within you; you just need to find ways to access it.

Don't be afraid of what others think of you. All that matters is what you think of yourself.

To sit with a dog on a hillside on a glorious afternoon is to be back in Eden, where doing nothing was not boring – it was peace. *Milan Kundera*

Examine your strengths and weaknesses calmly, for tranquillity is impossible without honesty.

Finding Tranquillity

Are tranquil places rare and far away, or are they all around us? Some people seem to walk through life in a cloud of calm, so why does tranquillity seem so elusive to so many of us?

People travel to wonder at the height of mountains, at the huge waves of the sea, at the long courses of rivers, at the vast compass of the ocean, at the circular motion of the stars; and they pass by themselves without wondering. *St Augustine*

Attune yourself to the pace of nature, as the natural world has infinite patience.

Have courage and learn to be patient, and you will find tranquillity in everything you do.

It is hard to remain calm when you are suffering, but tranquillity often helps heal your wounds.

Forget the past and live the present hour.

Sarah Knowles Bolton

Sometimes to find a calm place you must first walk through a storm.

Hard work often goes to waste when it is not the product of a tranquil mind.

Look up and not down; look forward and not back; look out and not in; and lend a hand. *E. E. Hale*

Problems tend to shrink in size when viewed with a calm eye.

Place lavender under your pillow for a good night's rest.

You do not need to leave your room.
Remain sitting at your table and
listen. Do not even listen, simply
wait, be quiet, still and solitary.
The world will freely offer itself to
you to be unmasked, it has no choice,
it will roll in ecstasy at your feet.

Franz Kafka

Those who are tranquil live longer than those who strive.

True tranquillity is a combination of acceptance and hope.

I shut my eyes in order to see. *Paul Gauguin*

Often the quickest way to find tranquillity is to turn away from stressful situations.

Force yourself to laugh now and then and you will often realize that things are not nearly as bad as they seem.

There may be something good in silence. It's a brand new thing. You can hear the funniest little discussions, if you keep turning the volume down. Shut yourself up, and listen out loud. *Wes Borland*

Close your eyes and allow your entire body to relax, from your eyebrows down to your toes. A fully relaxed body in turn leads to a relaxed mind.

Concentrate on one of your five senses and allow a smell, touch, taste, sight or sound to fill your world for a moment.

Running is a great way to relieve stress and clear the mind.
Joan Van Ark

Make sure staying calm is always at the top of your list of options.

Get off the bus or train one stop early and treat yourself to a short walk.

Take rest; a field that has rested gives a bountiful crop. *Ovid*

Let your mind wander, and try and block any conscious thoughts that come into your head.

Eat healthily and you'll feel better for it. In particular eat more alkaline foods than acidic foods.

If you follow your bliss, you put yourself on a kind of track that has been there all the while, waiting for you, and the life that you ought to be living is the one you are living. When you can see that, you begin to meet people who are in your field of bliss, and they open doors to you. I say, follow your bliss and don't be afraid, and doors will open where you didn't know they were going to be.

Joseph Campbell

Don't confuse tranquillity with taking the easy option. To be tranquil you must be true to yourself, which sometimes means making difficult decisions.

Keep a diary, and write down when you have felt stressed and when you have felt calm. Try and find patterns and then avoid the situations that threaten your tranquillity.

No one can get inner peace by pouncing on it.

Harry Emerson Fosdick

Tranquillity never finds those who are running away from themselves.

Treat problems as if they were ripples on the surface of the ocean, and imagine yourself being as still and calm as the waters on the sea bed.

Good humor is a tonic for mind and body. It is the best antidote for anxiety and depression. It is a business asset. It attracts and keeps friends. It lightens human burdens. It is the direct route to serenity and contentment.

Grenville Kleiser

Stop. Take a deep breath. Do this at least once every hour to maintain your tranquillity throughout the day.

Sit in a church for half an hour. It doesn't matter if you are not religious – sacred spaces are always peaceful places.

A happy life must be to a great extent a quiet life, for it is only in an atmosphere of quiet that true joy dare live.

Bertrand Russell

When you feel you know nothing, don't become frustrated but instead celebrate the mystery of life.

Practice using your imagination;
it can build beautiful tranquil places
for you whenever you need them.

**Arranging a bowl of flowers in the morning
can give a sense of quiet in a crowded day –
like writing a poem or saying a prayer.**
Anne Morrow Lindbergh

A positive outlook can turn envy into awe and frustration into patience.

Play is as important to adults as it is to children.

Sometimes I get up very early in the morning and enjoy a quiet house and cup of tea before the craziness begins. Other times, I'll take a quick walk on the beach. You can find peace in a few minutes.
Cindy Crawford

Sing to yourself, even if you're too shy to sing out loud. Songs lift the spirit and calm the heart.

Every now and then just go somewhere else. It doesn't have to be far from home – any change of scenery will help you to relax.

All men's miseries derive from not being able to sit in a quiet room alone.
Blaise Pascal

Write a list of the things that you associate with tranquillity and then try and include some of those things in your day to day routine.

Every night, I have to read a book, so that my mind will stop thinking about things that I stress about. *Britney Spears*

Engage with the natural world. Watching fish swim, birds fly or even spiders spinning webs all help relax the mind.

Learn to manage your stress levels.

Everybody should have his personal sounds to listen for – sounds that will make him exhilarated and alive or quiet and calm… One of the greatest sounds of them all – and to me it is a sound – is utter, complete silence.

André Kostelanetz

It is never 'the wrong time' to take a break.

Surround yourself with tranquil people and you will soon discover that tranquillity is contagious.

In the attitude of silence the soul finds the path in a clearer light, and what is elusive and deceptive resolves itself into crystal clearness. Our life is a long and arduous quest after Truth. *Mahatma Gandhi*

Take life a day at a time; problems seem more manageable that way.

Treat yourself to a massage.

God never did make a more calm, quiet, innocent recreation than angling.

Izaak Walton

Seek out the sea, a lake or even a small pond. Nothing relaxes us like water.

Take time out to watch the sunset at least once a week.

Curiosity endows the people who have it with a generosity in argument and a serenity in their own mode of life which springs from their cheerful willingness to let life take the form it will.

Alistair Cooke

Do nothing for at least an hour before you go to bed. You will find the time relaxing and you will sleep more soundly too.

Never be in a hurry; do everything quietly and in a calm spirit. Do not lose your inner peace for anything whatsoever, even if your whole world seems upset.

Saint Francis de Sales

Tranquillity is a type of freedom.

If your needs are few, finding tranquillity becomes a great deal easier.

It is interesting to notice how some minds seem almost to create themselves, springing up under every disadvantage, and working their solitary but irresistible way through a thousand obstacles.

Washington Irving

If you value tranquillity, choose to remain quiet rather than speak ill of others.

Patience and
fortitude are
the twin pillars
of inner peace.

The secret of success is to be in harmony with existence, to be always calm to let each wave of life wash us a little farther up the shore.
Cyril Connolly

Nothing gives you a sense of perspective like climbing mountains.

All too often what stands between a person and tranquillity is their own fear.

Silence is more musical than any song.

Christina Rossetti

Try growing something, even if it is only carrot tops in a saucer of water. Nurturing is a great way to relax.

But I do know focusing on the exterior doesn't make me happy. If I want peace and serenity, it won't be reached by getting thinner or fatter. *Elle Macpherson*

You must create tranquillity rather than searching for it.

Achieving tranquillity is often a matter of doing nothing.

Those who complain are rarely tranquil.

With the coming of spring, I am calm again. *Gustav Mahler*

Only those who truly know themselves can ever be tranquil.

Be still, and allow tranquillity to gradually soak into you.

Night, the beloved. Night, when words fade and things come alive. When the destructive analysis of day is done, and all that is truly important becomes whole and sound again. When man reassembles his fragmentary self and grows with the calm of a tree.

Antoine de Saint-Exupéry

Tranquillity cannot be separated from personal responsibility.

Relax your posture: if you are hunched and stiff you will feel tense on the inside as well as on the outside.

Silence is exhilarating at first – as noise is – but there is a sweetness to silence outlasting exhilaration, akin to the sweetness of listening and the velvet of sleep.

Edward Hoagland

Tranquillity is the art of feeling at home wherever you may be.

Lie down in the dark for a few minutes and many of your problems will melt away.

In every out-thrust headland, in every curving beach, in every grain of sand, there is the story of the earth.

Rachel Carson

Evolution changes the world more profoundly than revolution.

Try getting up an hour earlier than usual and savouring the quiet time before the rest of the world is awake.

If the blood humour is too strong and robust, calm it with balance and harmony.
Xun Zi

Every now and then, take your watch off and forget the time.

The language of tranquillity has to be learned in the same way as any other language has to be learned.

The final wisdom of life requires not the annulment of incongruity but the achievement of serenity within and above it.

Reinhold Niebuhr

Soak a towel in hot water and place it over your neck and shoulders.

Take regular short sips of water throughout the day.

The Arctic expresses the sum of all wisdom: Silence. *Walter Bauer*

Concentrate on treading gently when you walk.

Keep your home and work place tidy and you'll find they are more relaxing places to spend time in.

I began by doing physical yoga, initially just for the workout, as exercise. I would get peaceful and calm at the end of it, and I was curious about that.

Mariel Hemmingway

There are no barriers to tranquillity that cannot be overcome.

What is a television apparatus to man, who has only to shut his eyes to see the most inaccessible regions of the seen and the never seen, who has only to imagine in order to pierce through walls and cause all the planetary Baghdads of his dreams to rise from the dust.

Salvador Dalí

Nobody was born anxious. Anxiety is something we learn, and need to unlearn in order to find peace.

You find tranquillity by walking through the paper walls of fear.

Everybody's definition of tranquillity is different, and you will only really know tranquillity when you feel it.

Finding some quiet time in your life, I think, is hugely important.

Mariel Hemmingway

No matter where you are,
tranquillity is closer than you think.

**Though we often lose touch
with tranquillity, it never
loses touch with us.**

Don't concentrate on your
faults but on how you can
improve. Small, gradual
improvements pave the
way to tranquillity.

But being quiet and meditating on sound is something completely different and will be discovered very soon by a lot of people who feel that the visual world doesn't reach their soul anymore.

Karlheinz Stockhausen

The reason it seems hard to find tranquillity is not because it is rare but because it is difficult to recognize.

Don't be afraid to splash about in puddles like a child.

Every time I have some moment on a seashore, or in the mountains, or sometimes in a quiet forest, I think this is why the environment has to be preserved.
Bill Bradley

Gently massage your temples with your fingers whenever you feel stress getting the better of you.

I have never appreciated a quiet moment with a friend as much as a quiet moment with a book and I think part of that is my obsession with being older and time going faster and it's become increasingly sweeter for me.

Candice Bergen

Once a week, turn off every electrical appliance and rediscover what it is like to engage with the world using just your own senses.

Tranquillity does not have to be pure or perfect in order for you to enjoy it.

If we are too busy, if we are carried away every day by our projects, our uncertainty, our craving, how can we have the time to stop and look deeply into the situation – our own situation, the situation of our beloved one, the situation of our family and of our community, and the situation of our nation and of the other nations?

Thich Nhat Hanh

A sense of calm produces more energy than a sense of panic.

I love that quiet time when nobody's up and the animals are all happy to see me.
Olivia Newton-John

Demand nothing from life and life will reward you with the gift of tranquillity.

Kick off your shoes whenever you can. If you can go barefoot, so much the better.

I've travelled around the UK a lot recently and have discovered that I really like trains. If you're in the quiet carriage, nobody can get hold of you and you can relax.

Honor Blackman

Sometimes you have to sacrifice a little ambition in order to gain a large amount of peace.

When was the last time you spent a quiet moment just doing nothing – just sitting and looking at the sea, or watching the wind blowing the tree limbs, or waves rippling on a pond, a flickering candle or children playing in the park?

Ralph Marston

Be grateful for everything that life brings your way – even challenges and defeats. We often learn more about ourselves in adversity than we do when life is going well.

Time spent worrying is time that could be spent relaxing.

If you look for it, tranquillity is all around you, all of the time.

In reading, a lonely quiet concert is given to our minds; all our mental faculties will be present in this symphonic exaltation.

Stéphane Mallarmé

Tranquillity is as brittle or as strong as you are.

Rest is not idleness, and to lie sometimes on the grass under trees on a summer's day, listening to the murmur of the water, or watching the clouds float across the sky, is by no means a waste of time.

J. Lubbock

Tranquillity of the Heart

It is often those that we care about most who cause the most turbulence in our lives. Here we look at how to find, and keep, tranquillity within relationships.

Romance is tempestuous.
Love is calm. *Mason Cooley*

If you fill your heart with compassion then you will find your mind fills with tranquillity.

Everything in life is uncertain: accept this and you will ultimately feel more secure.

Walk away from confrontation and you will be walking towards tranquillity.

Fears feed fears; confidence breeds confidence.

If we would build on a sure foundation in friendship we must love friends for their sake rather than our own.

Charlotte Brontë

To enjoy tranquillity you must have enough room in your heart for it, so empty your heart of hatred or any other negative feelings.

The heart can sometimes be deceived, but it never lies.

To understand others and to feel understood by them – that is tranquillity.

The heart has its reasons that
reason does not know.
Pascal

**Occasionally a good cry helps release
an enormous amount of tension.**

Take your time over big decisions. Acting in haste often leads to trouble further down the line.

If you are constantly suspicious of others you will always be tense yourself.

It doesn't matter what the other is being, doing, having, saying, wanting, demanding. It doesn't matter what the other is thinking, expecting, planning. It only matters what you are being in relationship to that.

Neale Donald Walsch

Learn to trust, and reward those who trust in you, and you will have all the tranquillity you desire.

You must be in harmony with yourself before you can hope to be in harmony with the rest of the world.

Anyone can become angry – that is easy. But to be angry with the right person, to the right degree, at the right time, for the right purpose, and in the right way – this is not easy.

Aristotle

Accepting that things do not always go according to plan will help you to relax when they don't.

Follow the advice of those who have already found tranquillity.

Everything feels calmer by candlelight.

There is a sacredness in tears. They are not the mark of weakness, but of power. They speak more eloquently than ten thousand tongues. They are the messengers of overwhelming grief, of deep contrition, and of unspeakable love.

Washington Irving

Tranquil people rarely interfere in the lives of others.

Saying 'thank you' regularly opens the door of tranquillity.

A kiss is a lovely trick designed by nature to stop speech when words become superfluous.
Ingrid Bergman

If you give in to everyone who makes demands upon your time then you will leave no time for you to be yourself.

A smile attracts other smiles, and smiles in turn attract tranquillity.

A kind heart is a fountain of gladness, making everything in its vicinity freshen into smiles.
Washington Irving

Speak in a soft voice and you will find yourself using soft words.

Take regular exercise and you'll feel better not just physically but emotionally too.

Buy less. It might feel like 'treating yourself' to buy things you don't need, but actually cluttering up your life with material things becomes a barrier to tranquillity after a while.

Sharing is sometimes more demanding than giving. *Mary Catherine Bateson*

Phone a friend out of the blue just to see how they are.

Don't try and be perfect, and don't expect other people to be perfect either.

Apologize when you get something wrong. You'll feel better, and the person you apologize to will feel better too.

Civilization is a method of living and an attitude of equal respect for all people.
Jane Addams

Don't feel sorry for yourself: 99% of feeling tranquil is not about what happens to you, but how you react to what happens to you.

Have lunch with a friend. Eating 'on the go' is bad for digestion so make the time to eat properly.

Be calm in arguing; for fierceness makes error a fault, and truth discourtesy.

George Herbert

Be genuine, even if that means saying something you fear that others will not want to hear. You cannot find tranquillity by lying about who you are.

Join a new group dedicated to a subject or pastime that interests you.

For there is no friend like a sister in calm or stormy weather; To cheer one on the tedious way, to fetch one if one goes astray, to lift one if one totters down, to strengthen whilst one stands.

Christina Rossetti

Give your loved ones space, and demand space for yourself too.

Keep in regular contact with those you care about, even if it is only a text message.

Become a volunteer: helping others will make you feel good about yourself and you'll also make new friends.

But I'll tell you what hermits realize. If you go off into a far, far forest and get very quiet, you'll come to understand that you're connected with everything.

Alan Watts

Always make eye contact when you're talking with somebody. They will relax if they think you are interested in what they have to say, and this in turn will relax you.

In every group of friends, there is always one who tends to initiate get-togethers. Make sure you are that person for your group of friends.

If you have only one smile in you, give it to the people you love. Don't be surly at home, then go out in the street and start grinning 'Good morning' at total strangers. *Maya Angelou*

When you enjoy somebody's company, make sure that they know it. Send a thank you card or just give them a quick call to say how much you enjoyed meeting up with them.

Don't gossip. It won't win you any real friends, and it can cause serious conflicts further down the line.

No person is your friend who demands your silence, or denies your right to grow. *Alice Walker*

Learn how to keep a secret. A friend will not forgive you if something they tell you in confidence later becomes public knowledge.

Allow your loved ones to help you. It is good to be independent, but relationships are about give and take.

One important reason to stay calm is that calm parents hear more. Low-key, accepting parents are the ones whose children keep talking.

Mary Pipher

Don't harbour grudges: to be tranquil you must learn to forgive and forget.

Don't forget old friends when you acquire exciting new friends. If you're loyal you will receive loyalty in return and this will help you feel confident in times of trouble.

You see much more of your children once they leave home.
Lucille Ball

Try not to blur the boundaries between friends and lovers, or you may end up losing both a friend and a lover.

Making friends online can be a great comfort, but always value your 'real' relationships over your 'virtual' ones.

Learn to be quiet enough to hear the genuine within yourself so that you can hear it in others.

Marian Wright Edelman

Be there for your friends and family when they need you, but be careful not to let them crowd out your own life.

Sometimes you have to walk away from someone you love in order to find tranquillity, and you shouldn't feel guilty for doing so.

There's a magical tie to the land of our home, which the heart cannot break, though the footsteps may roam.
Eliza Cook

Warm your pajamas – and your loved one's if you have one – before retiring to bed.

Make at least one evening a week a TV-free evening.

Vows made in storms are forgotten in calm.

Thomas Fuller

An arm around the shoulder at the right time is one of the quickest paths to tranquillity.

True love means accepting that people change – and embracing that change rather than trying to prevent it.

I've deliberately tried to calm myself down because eventually I want to be a good role model to my kids.
Robbie Williams

Slip a little note or treat into a friend's pocket when they're not looking.

Compatibility isn't a matter of 'good chemistry': it is something you have to work at.

There are times when silence has the loudest voice.

Leroy Brownlow

**Infatuation leads to feelings of insecurity.
True love leads to a sense of calm.**

Self love, my liege, is not so vile a sin as self-neglecting.
William Shakespeare

In love there are no shortcuts.

Romantics are more tranquil than cynics.

I inherited that calm from my father, who was a farmer. You sow, you wait for good or bad weather, you harvest, but working is something you always need to do.

Miguel Indurain

In matters of the heart we are all amateurs, but if the only mistakes you make are genuine mistakes, you will always be forgiven by someone who truly loves you.

Good communication is vital in achieving tranquillity.

Show me the books he loves and I shall know the man far better than through mortal friends.

Dawn Adams

Don't dream of happy endings; work at making your relationships happy journeys.

Always give 100%, but never expect 100% in return.

Journey with me to a
true commitment to our
environment. Journey with
me to the serenity of leaving
to our children a planet in
equilibrium.
Paul Tsongas

If you're talkative by nature,
make a conscious effort to
listen more. If you're quiet by
nature, make a conscious effort
to open up a little more.

Those who care about you are not mind-readers, so make sure they know what they can do to help you.

What a lot we lost when we stopped writing letters. You can't reread a phone call.

Liz Carpenter

Routine is boring rather than tranquil. Be spontaneous.

Note down special occasions and anniversaries in your diary, and make the time to celebrate them.

Silence is the true friend that never betrays.
Confucius

Engagements with friends are as important as business meetings, so treat them accordingly.

Be prepared to make sacrifices for your loved ones, but don't allow yourself to become a martyr.

Before, I was so stupid. But, you know, when you have friends who died on the street, you say, okay, let's calm down. It's not the kind of energy I want to have in life. I want to go slower, and longer.

Olivier Martinez

Don't try and 'play it cool'. Be honest and open, and accept that what will be will be.

Never gloat when you are right, or sulk when you are wrong.

A man cannot be comfortable without his own approval.
Mark Twain

Don't try and pack all of your 'special time' into weekends. Try and find small amounts of tranquillity in each and every day.

It is great to feel comfortable in a relationship, but never let yourself get so comfortable that you start to take your partner for granted.

The seas are quiet when the winds give o'er; So calm are we when passions are no more!
Edmund Waller

Never use your love for someone as a bargaining chip.

Make a 'keepsake box' and fill it with reminders of happy times you have shared with your loved ones.

Love is the emblem of eternity; it confounds all notions of time; effaces all memory of beginning, all fear of an end.

Madame de Staël

In relationships, there is no tranquillity without equality.

It is not enough to simply tell yourself that your friends and family are your number 1 priority: your actions have to reflect this. Work overtime in your personal life and you'll be rewarded not with money but with harmony.

Silences make the real conversations between friends. Not the saying but the never needing to say is what counts.

Margaret Lee Runbeck

Love grows if you nurture it, and withers if you do not.

Re-read a favourite book or re-watch a favourite film.

I love children: especially when they cry, for then someone takes them away.
Nancy Mitford

Sharing your favourite food together is both relaxing and intimate. Close families always find the time to eat together.

Children learn by example: don't tell them to do one thing and then do another thing yourself.

Your days are short here; this is the last of your springs. And now in the serenity and quiet of this lovely place, touch the depths of truth, feel the hem of Heaven. You will go away with old, good friends. And don't forget when you leave why you came.

Adlai E. Stevenson

Act upon your feelings. Love is an emotion; romance is an action.

Small, genuine gestures are more meaningful than grand gestures that you feel obliged to make.

When all else is lost, the future still remains.

Christian Bovee

Allow your bedroom to be a place for romance and sleeping – and nothing else.

Take an afternoon off to go to the cinema.

Cultivate solitude and quiet and a few sincere friends, rather than mob merriment, noise and thousands of nodding acquaintances.
William Powell

Hugs cost nothing, so be generous in giving them to others.

Nothing feels quite as relaxing or indulgent as breakfast in bed.

Animals are such agreeable friends, they ask no questions, they pass no criticisms.
George Eliot

Emails and texts are convenient, but nothing tells someone you care like a letter does.

People do not commit to one another when they cease to have any doubts; they commit to one another when love overcomes their doubts.

After a storm comes a calm.
Matthew Henry

Time with a loved one is the most precious time of all, so ensure that time cannot be interrupted.

In relationships, celebrate not just your similarities but your differences too.

There is a fellowship more quiet even than solitude, and which, rightly understood, is solitude made perfect.

Robert Louis Stevenson

No matter how close you are to others, make sure your very best friend is you.

It is easy to be calm when agreeing with someone, but much harder to be calm when disagreeing with someone.

There should always, always be time in your life for your loved ones.

Until I accept my faults I will most certainly doubt my virtues.

Hugh Prather

Tranquillity at Work

Almost everybody feels under pressure in their workplace, so it is especially important to try and find tranquil moments amidst the daily grind.

Men for the sake of getting a living forget to live.

Margaret Fuller

Delegate whenever you can. You will place less pressure on yourself, and others will relish the faith you have placed in them.

Don't be tempted to use coffee as a 'pick-me-up' during the day.

Don't be tempted to use alcohol to 'wind down' after a hard day.

One of the symptoms of an approaching nervous breakdown is the belief that one's work is terribly important.

Bertrand Russell

Try taking exercise in your lunch hour, even if it is only a walk around the block.

Place soothing reminders of home around your work space.

The pursuit, even of the best things, ought to be calm and tranquil.

Marcus Tullius Cicero

Set yourself achievable goals each day, and celebrate when you meet your targets.

Make sure your office chair and desk are adjusted correctly, and get up and stretch at least once every hour.

The more tranquil a man becomes, the greater is his success, his influence, his power for good. Calmness of mind is one of the beautiful jewels of wisdom.

James Allen

Place fresh flowers in your workspace.

We all tend to 'over-breathe' when anxious, which only makes the symptoms of anxiety worse. Breathe in through your nose whilst counting to 3, then breathe out through your mouth whilst counting to 3. Continue breathing this way for 5 minutes and you should feel calmer.

Sometimes it's important to work for that pot of gold. But other times it's essential to take time off and to make sure that your most important decision in the day simply consists of choosing which colour to slide down on the rainbow.

Douglas Pagels

Change out of your work clothes as soon as you get home.

Make sure your work space is adequately lit, but not harshly lit.

Follow effective action with quiet reflection. From the quiet reflection will come even more effective action.

Peter Drucker

Bring an mp3 player to work and listen to relaxing music during your breaks.

Count to ten when things get on top of you. You are six times more likely to suffer from heart disease if you are persistently angry.

203

Being in control of your life and having realistic expectations about your day-to-day challenges are the keys to stress management, which is perhaps the most important ingredient to living a happy, healthy and rewarding life. *Marilu Henner*

Consider working flexi-time in order to break up your work routine.

People tend to be more abrupt when at work. Try not to take anything said to you in the work place personally.

If we have not quiet in our minds, outward comfort will do no more for us than a golden slipper on a gouty foot.

John Bunyan

Recognize the early signs of stress and act upon them to prevent stress overwhelming you.

If you feel work is getting you down, remind yourself what you are working for. Focusing on the rewards that work brings, rather than work itself, often helps to put things in perspective.

I have always been very calm on the outside. I'm not too stressed now just because I'm in Formula One. For me, tomorrow will be another day whether I finish first or last. I have to do the maximum and I cannot ask any more from myself.

Fernando Alonso

Don't bring your work home with you.

Try and talk to colleagues in person rather than sending emails or phoning them.

The only liberty an inferior man really cherishes is the liberty to quit work, stretch out in the sun, and scratch himself.
H.L. Mencken

If you have done your best then you should be satisfied, regardless of whether a particular project you were working on succeeded or failed.

Tidy up your work space before you leave work, so that when you return the next day you will start the day on the right note.

There's a lot more power in calm than in vituperation.

Dennis Prager

Every day is a great day,
even if it is a long day at work.

Focus on the possibilities of the future rather than worrying about the challenges it might bring.

If you can't pay for a thing, don't buy it. If you can't get paid for it, don't sell it. Do this, and you will have calm and drowsy nights, with all of the good business you have now and none of the bad. If you have time, don't wait for time.

Ernst Fischer

Have confidence in your own ability and difficulties will seem much smaller to you.

Don't just see opportunities, seize them.

I love deadlines. I like the whooshing sound they make as they fly by.
Douglas Adams

Enthusiasm leads to success; success leads to happiness and happiness leads to tranquillity.

Choose your battles carefully and don't waste energy tackling things you can never change.

We live longer than our forefathers; but we suffer more from a thousand artificial anxieties and cares. They fatigued only the muscles, we exhaust the finer strength of the nerves.

Edward George Bulwer-Lytton

Taking a break is not the same as quitting.

Do things well, even if you are on a tight schedule. If you rush jobs you will end up having to do them again eventually.

There's an hysterical, tired sense of humor that comes after working 14 hours a day, six days a week. I like those things because they take the pressure off the constant stress.

Tom Berenger

The more realistic your dreams
the fewer your nightmares.

Doing a job well will ultimately bring you more satisfaction than spending the money you were paid to do the job.

There is precious little hope to be got out of whatever keeps us industrious, but there is a chance for us whenever we cease work and become stargazers.

H.M. Tomlinson

Don't over-do it at Christmas parties, even if your colleagues are going wild. A single evening can cause embarrassment and stress for years.

The most powerful and respected leaders are those who can remain calm under pressure.

A life spent in constant labour is a life wasted, save a man be such a fool as to regard a fulsome obituary notice as ample reward.

George Jean Nathan

Success at work is worth nothing if it comes at the expense of happiness at home.

Always be punctual and you will avoid getting off on the wrong foot with people.

Yesterday is gone. Tomorrow has not yet come. We have only today. Let us begin.
Mother Teresa

Put work out of your mind when you are at home. You will be more productive if you come at problems fresh rather than constantly turning them over in your mind.

Sometimes hanging on in there is all you need to do.

It does not matter how slowly you go, so long as you do not stop.

Confucius

Try not to travel in rush-hour. Nothing is as frustrating as sitting in traffic.

Don't fall to pieces just because you're under a little pressure. Pressure is what turns coal into diamonds.

Now and then, bring treats into work and share them with your colleagues.

What isn't tried won't work. *Claude McDonald*

Work is important, but it should never be your whole life. Remind yourself every day of the life you have outside of work.

Nothing in the world can take the place of persistence. Talent will not; nothing is more common than unsuccessful men with talent. Genius will not; unrewarded genius is almost a proverb. Education will not; the world is full of educated derelicts. Persistence and determination alone are omnipotent. The slogan 'press on' has solved and always will solve the problems of the human race.

Calvin Coolidge

Tranquillity
of the Soul

There is little point journeying to remote idyllic places if we take our troubles with us. How do we find that true, deep, inner peace that lies within us?

In quiet moments when you think about it, you recognize what is critically important in life and what isn't. Be wise and don't let good things crowd out those that are essential.

Richard G. Scott

Tranquillity is the sense of feeling at one with the distant stars that gave birth to you.

If you treat every day as a precious gift it is almost impossible not to feel tranquil.

Sometimes you have to turn off your mind in order to hear your soul whisper to you.

Only by much searching and mining are gold and diamonds obtained, and man can find every truth connected with his being if he will dig deep into the mine of his soul.
James Allen

Listen to the birds singing at dawn and imagine they are singing to encourage you to make the very best of your day.

Peace starts with letting go. Remember that sometimes you have to un-learn bad old habits before you can develop good new habits.

To feel tranquillity you must learn to listen when the universe speaks.

Before you try and change the world, try changing the way you see the world.

The world renews itself every day, and if you allow it to then it can renew your soul every day too.

Seeking out quiet places helps, but in the end all peace, harmony and tranquillity comes from within.

Not merely an absence of noise, Real Silence begins when a reasonable being withdraws from the noise in order to find peace and order in his inner sanctuary.

Peter Minard

Seen from space, planet earth appears fragile, beautiful and tranquil. Keep this image in your mind when you are feeling stressed and frustrated.

Embrace change. You cannot grow without changing.

Bad things will happen from time to time, but you will only ever become a victim if you first choose to see yourself as one.

Contemplating problems is not the same as worrying: learn to tell the difference.

Words, words, words! They shut one off from the universe. Three quarters of the time one's never in contact with things, only with the beastly words that stand for them. *Aldous Huxley*

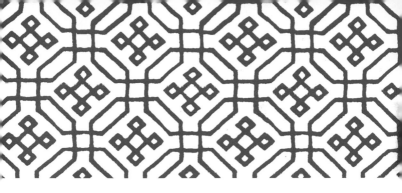

The Taoist Chuang Tzu once dreamt he was a butterfly, and then upon awaking wondered if he was actually a butterfly who was dreaming of being a man. We all build our own worlds in our minds, so make sure your mind is full of positive thoughts.

Tranquillity is about expanding into, not shrinking from, the universe that you are a part of.

Don't fall into the trap of thinking you don't have time to stop and relax. The busier you are the more important finding moments of tranquillity becomes.

It is useless to force the rhythms of life. If I live with the anxiety to go fast, I will not live well. My addiction to speed will make me sick. The art of living is about learning how to give time to each and every thing. If I have sacrificed my life to speed, then that is impossible. Ultimately, slow means to take the time to reflect. It means to take the time to think. With calm, you arrive everywhere.

Carlos Petrini

Now is always the time to tell yourself that here is where you belong.

Tranquillity is everywhere for those who are receptive to it.

The most important things in life are beyond language or explanation.

The components of anxiety, stress, fear, and anger do not exist independently of you in the world. They simply do not exist in the physical world, even though we talk about them as if they do.

Wayne Dyer

Tranquillity is found when you stop searching for it.

In our desire to find answers, we often make simple things more complicated than they need to be.

The material world is not life,
but only one part of life.

**Quietude, which some
men cannot abide because
it reveals their inward
poverty, is as a palace
of cedar to the wise, for
along its hallowed courts
the King in his beauty
deigns to walk.**
Charles H. Spurgeon

The power of the imagination allows us to float along a gentle stream even when we are riding a bus through a busy city.

We only know what courage is because of the challenges that sometimes require us to find it.

Learn to get in touch with the silence within yourself and know that everything in this life has a purpose.
Elisabeth Kübler-Ross

Confronting problems causes them to shrink; ignoring problems causes them to grow.

If you value yourself you will take better care of yourself.

When Mozart was composing at the end of the eighteenth century, the city of Vienna was so quiet that fire alarms could be given verbally, by a shouting watchman mounted on top of St. Stefan's Cathedral. In twentieth-century society, the noise level is such that it keeps knocking our bodies out of tune and out of their natural rhythms. This ever-increasing assault of sound upon our ears, minds, and bodies adds to the stress load of civilized beings trying to live in a highly complex environment. *Steven Halpern*

Often we do not see the real world, but the reflection of ourselves in the world.

Heaven and hell are not above and below us. We carry them in our hearts.

By all means be self-critical, but remember to praise yourself sometimes too.

For no art and no religion is possible until we make allowances, until we manage to keep quiet the enfant terrible of logic that plays havoc with the other faculties.

John C. Ransom

We find the answers to life by living, not by thinking.

There is no one meaning to life; we each have to find our own meaning.

Soon silence will have passed into legend. Man has turned his back on silence. Day after day he invents machines and devices that increase noise and distract humanity from the essence of life, contemplation, meditation… tooting, howling, screeching, booming, crashing, whistling, grinding, and trilling bolster his ego. His anxiety subsides. His inhuman void spreads monstrously like a gray vegetation.

Jean Arp

Take control of your thoughts rather than letting your thoughts control you.

Every single person you meet can teach you something about yourself.

Tranquillity cannot be seen, heard, or touched, yet it lies waiting for us within everything we see, hear, and touch.

With an eye made quiet by the power of harmony, and the deep power of joy, we see into the life of things.

William Wordsworth

Listen to the opinions of others, but never let them override your own judgement.

Nobody is perfect, thank goodness.

There is a theory which states that if ever anyone discovers exactly what the Universe is for and why it is here, it will instantly disappear and be replaced by something even more bizarre and inexplicable. There is another theory which states that this has already happened. *Douglas Adams*

Taking the easy option rarely leads to peace.

Make leaving the world a better place your only goal.

Lives are changed by a moment's listening to conscience, by a single and quiet inclination of the mind.

George A. Smith

To find tranquillity you have to be ruthless in weeding out distractions.

If you only ever focus on surviving you will leave no time for living.

Peace is not a relationship of nations. It is a condition of mind brought about by a serenity of soul. Peace is not merely the absence of war. It is also a state of mind. Lasting peace can come only to peaceful people.

Jawaharlal Nehru

No job is more important than the job of finding inner peace.

Every day is a fresh start and a clean slate.

It suddenly struck me that that tiny pea, pretty and blue, was the Earth. I put up my thumb and shut one eye, and my thumb blotted out the planet Earth. I didn't feel like a giant. I felt very, very small. *Neil Armstrong*

Be kind. Whatever you do to others is ultimately what you do to yourself.

Tranquillity doesn't come easily – it requires commitment, dedication and practice.

Never take tranquillity for granted. Store it within your heart so that you can tap into it when you most need it.

To see things in the seed, that is genius. *Lao Tzu*

Tranquil Lives

Words of advice from those who have found tranquillity – and a few who have lost it. From the light-hearted to the profound, there is bound to be something to cheer or inspire in this section.

Retire into yourself as much as possible.
Seneca

Of any stopping place in life, it is good to ask whether it will be a good place from which to go on as well as a good place to remain.
Mary Catherine Bateson

The field of consciousness is tiny. It accepts only one problem at a time.
Antoine de Saint-Exupéry

Great events make me quiet and calm; it is only trifles that irritate my nerves.

Queen Victoria

All noise is waste. So cultivate quietness in your speech, in your thoughts, in your emotions. Speak habitually low. Wait for attention and then your low words will be charged with dynamite.

Elbert Hubbard

The life of inner peace, being harmonious and without stress, is the easiest type of existence.

Norman Vincent Peale

Accustomed to the veneer of noise, to the shibboleths of promotion, public relations, and market research, society is suspicious of those who value silence.

John Lahr

What I dream of is an art of balance, of purity and serenity devoid of troubling or depressing subject matter – a soothing, calming influence on the mind, rather like a good armchair which provides relaxation from physical fatigue.

Henri Matisse

The best cure for the body is a quiet mind.
Napoléon Bonaparte

I'm not afraid of storms, for I'm learning to sail my ship.

Louisa May Alcott

Few things are brought to a successful issue by impetuous desire, but most by calm and prudent forethought.

Thucydides

The world is never quiet, even its silence eternally resounds with the same notes, in vibrations which escape our ears. As for those that we perceive, they carry sounds to us, occasionally a chord, never a melody.

Albert Camus

Time is a dressmaker specializing in alterations.

Faith Baldwin

The talkative parrot is shut up in a cage. Other birds, without speech, fly freely about.

Saskya Pandita

He who is of calm and happy nature will hardly feel the pressure of age, but to him who is of an opposite disposition youth and age are equally a burden.

Plato

You grow up the day you have your first real laugh at yourself.
Ethel Barrymore

Remain calm, serene, always in command of yourself. You will then find out how easy it is to get along.
Paramahansa Yogananda

If a man will begin with certainties, he shall end in doubts, but if he will be content to begin with doubts, he shall end in certainties. *Francis Bacon*

Talk that does not end in any kind of action is better suppressed altogether.
Thomas Carlyle

The fragrance always stays in the hand that gives the rose.

Hada Bejar

It was only from an inner calm that man was able to discover and shape calm surroundings.

Stephen Gardiner

Nothing is more useful than silence.

Menander of Athens

Many a calm river begins as a turbulent waterfall, yet none hurtles and foams all the way to the sea. *Mikhail Lermontov*

Our faith in the present dies out long before our faith in the future.
Ruth Benedict

You'll never have a quiet world
till you knock the patriotism out
of the human race.
George Bernard Shaw

Happiness is good health
and a bad memory.
Ingrid Bergman

He who seldom speaks, and with one calm well-timed word can strike dumb the loquacious, is a genius or a hero.
Johann Kaspar Lavater

Everybody needs beauty as well as bread, places to play in and pray in, where nature may heal and give strength to body and soul. *John Muir*

The good and the wise lead quiet lives. *Euripides*

Certainty is the mother of quiet and repose, and uncertainty the cause of variance and contentions.

Edward Coke

Birds sing after a storm; why shouldn't people feel as free to delight in whatever remains to them?

Rose Kennedy

People are never quiet. It's go, go, go. I'm a go-getter, but you need rest and silence, just to sit around and think about things. *Dana Hill*

In struggling against anguish one never produces serenity; the struggle against anguish only produces new forms of anguish. *Simone Weil*

Cows are amongst the gentlest of breathing creatures; none show more passionate tenderness to their young when deprived of them; and, in short, I am not ashamed to profess a deep love for these quiet creatures.

Thomas de Quincey

The brain is not, and cannot be, the sole or complete organ of thought and feeling.
Alice Stone Blackwell

Now all my teachers are dead except silence.

W.S. Merwin

Age is something that doesn't matter, unless you are a cheese. *Billie Burke*

Power is so characteristically calm, that calmness in itself has the aspect of strength. *Edward Bulwer-Lytton*

Sooner or later you learn that you belong in the big leagues, and that makes you calm down.
Dennis Eckersley

A garden must combine the poetic and the mysterious with a feeling of serenity and joy.
Luis Barragán

Remember the quiet wonders. The world has more need of them than it has for warriors.

Charles de Lint

The healthy being craves an occasional wildness, a jolt from normality, a sharpening of the edge of appetite, his own little festival of Saturnalia, a brief excursion from his way of life.

Robert MacIver

You know, the men go to tea houses with the expectation that they will have a nice quiet evening and not read about it the next morning in the newspaper. **Arthur Golden**

I moved to New York City for my health.
I'm paranoid and New York was the only
place where my fears were justified.
Anita Weiss

Life being very short, and the
quiet hours of it few, we ought to
waste none of them in reading
valueless books. *John Ruskin*

I don't think necessity is the mother of invention. Invention, in my opinion, arises directly from idleness, possibly also from laziness – to save oneself trouble. *Agatha Christie*

The deepest rivers make least din, the silent soule doth most abound in care. *William Alexander*

One's age should be tranquil, as childhood should be playful. Hard work at either extremity of life seems out of place. At midday the sun may burn, and men labour under it; but the morning and evening should be alike calm and cheerful. *Thomas Arnold*

In this world without quiet corners, there can be no easy escapes from history, from hullabaloo, from terrible, unquiet fuss. **Salman Rushdie**

Life is a mystery as deep as ever death can be.

Mary Mapes Dodge

A wise man adapts himself to circumstances as water shapes itself to the vessel that contains it.

Chinese proverb

Besides the noble art of getting things done, there is the noble art of leaving things undone. The wisdom of life consists in the elimination of non-essentials. *Lin Yutang*

The poet is willing to stop anywhere… And it's that willingness to slow down and examine the mysterious bits of fluff in our lives that is the poet's interest. *William Collins*

A poor life this if,
full of care,
We have no time to
stand and stare.

William Henry Davies

**I sometimes suspect that half
our difficulties are imaginary
and that if we kept quiet about
them they would disappear.**

Robert Lynd

Real joy comes not from ease or riches or from the praise of others, but from doing something worthwhile. *Wilfred Grenfell*

Nothing is worth more than this day.
Johann Wolfgang von Goethe

Dream as if you'll live forever. Live as if you'll die today.
James Dean

The third-rate mind is only happy when it is thinking with the majority. The second-rate mind is only happy when it is thinking with the minority. The first-rate mind is only happy when it is thinking.

A. A. Milne

What we think, or what we know, or what we believe is, in the end, of little consequence. The only consequence is what we do. ***John Ruskin***

It's good to shut up sometimes.

Marcel Marceau

In quiet places, reason abounds.

Adlai E. Stevenson

There is a great difference between worry and concern. A worried person sees a problem, and a concerned person solves a problem.

Harold Stephens

Nowadays most men lead lives of noisy desperation.
James Thurber

Everyone thinks of changing the world, but no one thinks of changing himself.
Leo Tolstoy

You don't have to have fought in a war to love peace.

Geraldine Ferraro

The language of excitement is at best picturesque merely. You must be calm before you can utter oracles.

Henry David Thoreau

I'm full of fears and I do my best to avoid difficulties and any kind of complications. I like everything around me to be clear as crystal and completely calm.

Alfred Hitchcock

No pen, no ink,
no table, no room,
no time, no quiet,
no inclination.

James Joyce

Throughout my life I have learnt that when you're in the serious situations, you've got to try to stay calm. Because that's the way you get out of them.

John Newcombe

You want to be a writer, don't know how or when? Find a quiet place, use a humble pen.

Paul Simon

A happy life is just a string of happy moments.
But most people don't allow the happy moment, because they're so busy trying to get a happy life.

Esther Hicks

Stress is nothing more than a socially acceptable form of mental illness.
Richard Carlson

There is only one way to happiness and that is to cease worrying about things which are beyond the power of our will. *Epitectus*

I need something to do when I'm not working, or I crawl up the walls. So I've just taken up kung fu. I was looking for some kind of calming, relaxing activity. I tried yoga, but it wasn't really me.
Ian Hart

Climb the mountains and get their good tidings.
John Muir

You cannot shake hands with a clenched fist.

Indira Gandhi

When a house is being built which is to be made as strong as possible, the building takes place in fine weather and in calm, so that nothing may hinder the structure from acquiring the needed solidity.

Origen

Another thing I like to do is sit back and take in nature. To look at the birds, listen to their singing, go hiking, camping and jogging and running, walking along the beach, playing games and sometimes being alone with the great outdoors. It's very special to me. *Larry Wilcox*

I have more zits now than I did as a teenager. Stress zits.
Tiffani-Amber Thiessen

I don't know what my path is yet. I'm just walking on it.

Olivia Newton-John

I have learned silence from the talkative, toleration from the intolerant, and kindness from the unkind; yet, strange, I am ungrateful to those teachers.

Khalil Gibran

When I can look life in the eyes, grown calm and very coldly wise, life will have given me the truth, and taken in exchange – my youth. *Sara Teasdale*

The moment one gives close attention to anything, even a blade of grass, it becomes a mysterious, awesome, indescribably magnificent world in itself. ***Henry Miller***

**Silence is as deep as eternity;
speech, shallow as time.**
Thomas Carlyle

All truly great thoughts are
conceived by walking.
Friedrich Nietzsche

A liberal is a man or a woman or a child who looks forward to a better day, a more tranquil night, and a bright, infinite future.
Leonard Bernstein

I have often lamented that we cannot close our ears with as much ease as we can our eyes.
Richard Steele

Fortunately, psychoanalysis is not the only way to resolve inner conflicts. Life itself remains a very effective therapist.

Karen Horney

In the midst of winter, I found there was within me an invincible summer. *Albert Careb*

Life's under no obligation to give us what we expect.

Margaret Mitchell

There are some things you learn best in calm, and some in storm.

Willa Cather

And this, our life, exempt from public haunt, finds tongues in trees, books in the running brooks, sermons in stones, and good in everything.
William Shakespeare

I can live with doubt and uncertainty and not knowing. I think it is much more interesting to live not knowing than to have answers that might be wrong.
Richard Feynman

The best translations cannot convey to us the strength and exquisite delicacy of thought in its native garb, and he to whom such books are shut flounders about in outer darkness.

Edwin Booth

Nobody sees a flower really, it is so small. We haven't time, and to see takes time – like to have a friend takes time.

Georgia O'Keeffe

Silence is a source of great strength.
Lao Tzu

I have tremendous faith in the universe. I feel at home on this planet. Even though it's a very big world out there, I plan on walking right through the middle of it unharmed. *Marion Ross*

**New York has a trip-hammer vitality
which drives you insane with restlessness
if you have no inner stabilizer.**
Henry Miller

Happiness is the absence of striving for happiness.
Zhuangzi

I think that the ideal space must contain elements of magic, serenity, sorcery and mystery. *Luis Barragán*

To be 'on edge,' you are literally not centred – not being in your spiritual centre. *Carrie Latet*

The sole art that suits me is that which, rising from unrest, tends toward serenity.

André Gide

A morning-glory at my window satisfies me more than the metaphysics of books.

Walt Whitman

Trying to determine what is going on in the world by reading newspapers is like trying to tell the time by watching the second hand of a clock. *Ben Hecht*

To play well you must feel tranquil and at peace. I have never been troubled by nerves in golf because I felt I had nothing to lose and everything to gain.

Harry Vardon

All the problems of the world can be solved in a garden.

Geoff Lawton

Tranquil pleasures last the longest; we are not fitted to bear the burden of great joys.

Christian Nestell Bovee

It is good to have an end to journey towards; but it is the journey that matters in the end.

Ursula Le Guin

I like a very dark house, just black. I sit there and just think. Once I'm still and quiet inside, I'll begin. It's very personal; it has to be. One song may be Bach, the next blues, a song from TV, or a nursery rhyme or jazz piece.

Bobby McFerrin

We think a happy life consists in tranquillity of mind.

Marcus Tullius Cicero

Everybody's talking trash these days, so why not keep quiet? **Dennis Rodman**

Almost all our faults are more pardonable than the methods we resort to to hide them.

François de La Rochefoucauld

Music itself is a great source of relaxation. Parts of it anyway. Working in the studio, that's not relaxing, but playing an instrument that I don't know how to play is unbelievably relaxing, because I don't have any pressure on me.

Jackson Browne

Silence is the universal refuge, the sequel to all dull discourses and all foolish acts, a balm to our every chagrin, as welcome after satiety as after disappointment.
Henry David Thoreau

The most intense conflicts, if overcome, leave behind a sense of security and calm that is not easily disturbed. It is just these intense conflicts and their conflagration which are needed to produce valuable and lasting results. ***Carl Jung***

I'm sick of not having the courage to be an absolute nobody. I'm sick of myself and everybody else that wants to make some kind of a splash.

J.D. Salinger

I know the joy of fishes in the river through my own joy, as I go walking along the same river.

Zhuangzi

I'm not very good at relaxing. Reading's the main thing. On the bus, on the tube, on the loo. Literally all the time. I mean, I don't think there's a moment of the day when I wouldn't be if I was left alone.

Samuel West

Like water which can clearly mirror the sky and the trees only so long as its surface is undisturbed, the mind can only reflect the true image of the Self when it is tranquil and wholly relaxed. *Indra Devi*

I need to go someplace faraway
that doesn't have telephones and
doesn't have a record player and
doesn't have movie theaters and
people walking down the street
in order to not do anything.

Will Oldham

A mind at peace, a mind centred and not focused on harming others, is stronger than any physical force in the universe.
Wayne Dyer

A crust eaten in peace is better than a banquet partaken in anxiety.

Aesop

Ill fortune never crushed that man whom good fortune deceived not. *Francis Bacon*

I do pottery. I love it. It's very relaxing; it takes me to another planet. *Eva Herzigová*

Take a course in good water and air; and in the eternal youth of Nature you may renew your own. Go quietly, alone; no harm will befall you. **John Muir**

I started walking at night with my sister-in-law which has been amazing. It really does something for you. It just kind of clears the mind, it just makes you feel better, things start to tighten a little bit. *Ashley Scott*

Silence is a sounding thing, to one who listens hungrily.

Gwendolyn Bennett

An inability to stay quiet is one of the most conspicuous failings of mankind.
Walter Bagehot

All of us might wish at times that we lived in a more tranquil world, but we don't. And if our times are difficult and perplexing, so are they challenging and filled with opportunity.
Robert Kennedy

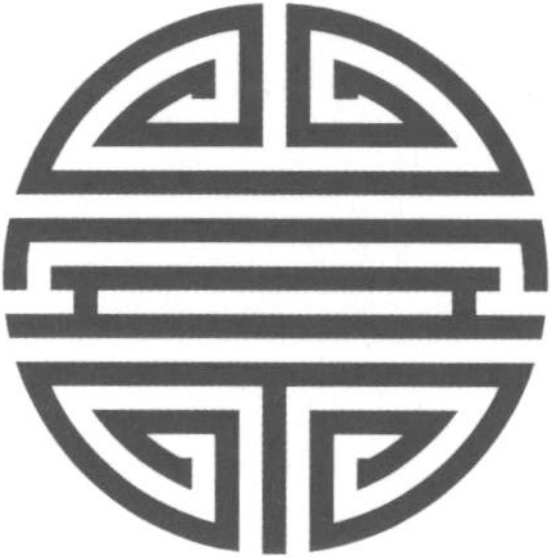

Staying
Tranquil

Tranquillity is notoriously fragile; it can be lost in the blink of an eye. So how do we protect our hard-won sense of calm, and how do we restore it if we lose it?

With increased opportunity comes increased stress. The stress comes from multiple conflicting demands and very little in the way of role models.
Madeline Hemmings

It is entirely natural to feel angry and frustrated sometimes. Indeed letting your anger out is the only way to restore your equilibrium.

When things go wrong, don't look for someone to blame. Spend your time making things right again instead.

Learn to forgive – both others and yourself.

Retain your sense of humour.

Self-pity in its early stages is as snug as a feather mattress. Only when it hardens does it become uncomfortable.

Maya Angelou

Accept help when it is offered, but never depend entirely on someone else.

It is far better to try and fail than never to try at all.

Offering encouragement to others often leads to you encouraging yourself too.

Aerodynamically the bumblebee shouldn't be able to fly, but the bumblebee doesn't know that so it goes on flying anyway.

Mary Kay Ash

It is when the situation is negative that a positive outlook is most useful.

Don't ignore the facts – change them.

Keep looking towards the future. Nothing is as corrosive to tranquillity as regret.

Stress is basically a disconnection from the earth, a forgetting of the breath. Stress is an ignorant state. It believes that everything is an emergency. Nothing is that important. Just lie down.

Natalie Goldberg

Always hope for the best but plan for the worst.

Don't be ashamed of failure: if you resolve to learn from your mistakes then failure can become your greatest teacher.

True friendships are often forged in the midst of shared adversity.

No matter how big or soft or warm your bed is, you still have to get out of it. *Grace Slick*

You can't please everyone all of the time.

Whenever you get down about how things are, focus on what things have the potential to become.

The best way to avenge those who harm you is to thrive.

Not a shred of evidence exists in favor of the idea that life is serious. *Brendan Gill*

It is when others doubt you that you most need faith in yourself.

Accept that you don't always get what you deserve, at least in the short term.

Within every challenge there is also a fresh opportunity.

Each day should have a clearly marked emergency exit sign.

Dr. Sun Wolf

Lashing out at others when things go wrong only makes matters worse.

Your true friends will help you when things look bleak, so don't be too proud to turn to them.

You cannot change the past, but you can learn from it to build a better future.

Courage is the price that life exacts for granting peace. The soul that knows it not, knows no release from little things; knows not the livid loneliness of fear.

Amelia Earhart

Don't retreat into your shell just because you have had a setback. Dust yourself down and come out fighting.

Sometimes your best isn't good enough – but remember that all you can ever do is your best.

The rays of happiness,
like those of light,
are colourless
when unbroken.

Henry W. Longfellow

**Never underestimate
your capacity to turn
things around.**

Be prepared to change your approach, but don't compromise on your values in order to get yourself out of a difficult situation.

If you never quit then you can never really lose.

The gem cannot be polished without friction, nor man be perfected without trials.

Danish proverb

Don't get angry with yourself. Calmly look at what you need to change about yourself in order to do better next time.

Keep the faith. You will only have lost everything when you have lost hope.

Don't be afraid to retrace your steps and try a different route.

In times of life crisis, whether wild fires or smoldering stress, the first thing I do is go back to basics… am I eating right, am I getting enough sleep, am I getting some physical and mental exercise everyday?

Edward Albert

When you feel lost, surround yourself with familiar things until you get your spiritual bearings again.

The world needs the rain just as much as it needs the sun.

I wonder what it is in the New York air that enables me to sit up till all hours of the night in an atmosphere which in London would make a horse dizzy, but here merely clears the brain.

James Agate

Never use alcohol or drugs as a crutch in times of trouble.

The more difficult your goals are to achieve, the more satisfying they will be when you ultimately achieve them.

There is a way to look at the past. Don't hide from it. It will not catch you if you don't repeat it. *Pearl Bailey*

Nobody has all of the answers. Settle for asking the right questions.

You will never find out who you really are unless you are prepared to risk failing at something.

Keep calm and carry on.

Wherever we look upon this earth, the opportunities take shape within the problems.

Nelson A. Rockefeller

Thinking negatively only makes problems worse.

Focus not on what you have lost but on what you still have.

Getting away from it all can give you a fresh perspective. Running away from it all will only bring more problems further down the line.

Everything that irritates us about others can lead us to an understanding of ourselves. *Carl Jung*

No matter how great the problem you are facing, promise yourself you will not think about it after a certain time in the evening. Losing sleep through worrying will not help you or those around you.

Check your goals are realistic. If you try and achieve the impossible you will be endlessly disappointed.

Being able to laugh at ourselves is important. A disaster is easier to cope with if you can turn it into a farce.

Its not stress that kills us, it is our reaction to it.

Hans Selye

Remember that you will never truly appreciate the highs of life unless you have also experienced the lows.

Tranquillity does not come when you feel successful, it comes when you feel satisfied: learn to tell the difference.

The best remedy for those who are afraid, lonely or unhappy is to go outside, somewhere where they can be quiet, alone with the heavens, nature and God. Because only then does one feel that all is as it should be.

Anne Frank

The
Tranquil
Smile

Being able to laugh at life is key to unwinding. Kick off your shoes and enjoy the wit of those who have sought, found and lost tranquillity throughout the ages.

How beautiful it is to do nothing, and then to rest afterward.
Spanish proverb

Reality is the leading cause of stress among those in touch with it.
Lily Tomlin

If you ask what is the single most important key to longevity, I would have to say it is avoiding worry, stress and tension. And if you didn't ask me, I'd still have to say it.

George Burns

The world is moving so fast these days that the one who says it can't be done is generally interrupted by someone doing it.

Harry Emerson Fosdick

Don't panic.

Douglas Adams

A vacation frequently means that the family goes away for a rest, accompanied by a mother who sees that the others get it.

Marcelene Cox

The object of opening the mind, as of opening the mouth, is to shut it again on something solid.

G.K. Chesterton

A bee is never as busy as it seems; it's just that it can't buzz any slower.

Kin Hubbard

If people concentrated on the really important things in life, there'd be a shortage of fishing poles.

Doug Larson

I try to take one day at a time, but sometimes several days attack me at once. *Jennifer Yane*

Death is nature's way of telling you to slow down.

There's never enough time to do all the nothing you want.

Bill Watterson

The man who doesn't relax and hoot a few hoots voluntarily, now and then, is in great danger of hooting hoots and standing on his head for the edification of the pathologist and trained nurse, a little later on.

Elbert Hubbard

We are so vain that we even care for the opinions of those we don't care for.
Marie Egner von Eschenbach

I like work; it fascinates me. I can sit and look at it for hours.

Jerome K. Jerome

Loafing needs no explanation and is its own excuse.

Christopher Morley

Till I was 13, I thought my name was 'Shut Up.' *Joe Namath*

Adam and Eve had an ideal marriage. He didn't have to hear about all the men she could have married, and she didn't have to hear about the way his mother cooked. **Kimberly Broyles**

Authors like cats because they are such quiet, lovable, wise creatures, and cats like authors for the same reasons.

Robertson Davies

I don't feel old. I don't feel anything until noon. Then it's time for my nap.

Bob Hope

I don't even butter my bread; I consider that cooking. *Katherine Cebrian*

We spend the first twelve months of our children's lives teaching them to walk and talk and the next twelve telling them to sit down and shut up.
Phyllis Diller

I feel that if a person has problems communicating the very least he can do is to shut up. *Tom Lehrer*

Most people are so busy knocking themselves out trying to do everything they think they should do, they never get around to what they want to do.

Kathleen Winsor

The best cure for insomnia is to get a lot of sleep.

W. C. Fields.

It is not enough to be busy. So are the ants. The question is: What are we busy about?

Henry David Thoreau

There is a fine line between fishing and just standing on the shore like an idiot.

Steven Wright

When everything seems to be going against you, remember that the airplane takes off against the wind, not with it.

Henry Ford

Sometimes you're the windshield; sometimes you're the bug.
Mark Knopfler

Isn't it strange how 'rush hour' is the time when nothing moves?

The place is very well and quiet and the children only scream in a low voice.
Lord Byron

Sometimes the most important thing in a whole day is the rest we take between two deep breaths.

Etty Hillesum

Cleaning your house while your kids are still growing is like shoveling the walk before it stops snowing.

Phyllis Diller

There is nothing so annoying as to have two people talking when you're busy interrupting.

Mark Twain

Smooth seas do not make skilful sailors.

African proverb

Honk if you hate noise pollution.

The world is full of fools; and he who would not wish to see one, must not only shut himself up alone, but must also break his looking-glass.

Nicolas Boileau

The really idle man gets nowhere. The perpetually busy man does not get much further.

Sir Heneage Ogilvie

There are an enormous number of managers who have retired on the job.
Peter Drucker

How many things are there which I do not want.

Socrates

Try to relax and enjoy the crisis.
Ashleigh Brilliant

I go about looking at horses and cattle. They eat grass, make love, work when they have to, bear their young. I am sick with envy of them.

Sherwood Anderson

I cannot always control what is going on around me but I can always control what I think about what is going on around me.

Lucy MacDonald

Some of the secret joys of living are not found by rushing from point A to point B, but by inventing some imaginary letters along the way. *Douglas Pagels*

Don't underestimate the value of Doing Nothing, of just going along, listening to all the things you can't hear, and not bothering. *A. A. Milne*

Reality is frequently inaccurate.

Douglas Adams

Parents are not interested in justice, they're interested in peace and quiet.
Bill Cosby

For fast-acting relief, try slowing down.
Lily Tomlin

Too often, the opportunity knocks, but by the time you push back the chain, push back the bolt, unhook the two locks and shut off the burglar alarm, it's too late.

Rita Coolidge

The mark of a successful man is one that has spent an entire day on the bank of a river without feeling guilty about it.

When I was born I was so surprised I didn't talk for a year and a half.
Gracie Allen

Spring is when you feel like whistling even with a shoe full of slush.

Doug Larson

The trouble with simple living
is that, though it can be joyful,
rich, and creative, it isn't simple.
Doris Janzen Longacre

**You may not realize
it when it happens,
but a kick in the teeth
may be the best thing
in the world for you.**
Walt Disney

If a man insisted always on being serious, and never allowed himself a bit of fun or relaxation, he would go mad or become unstable without knowing it.

Herodotus

The first sign of maturity is the discovery that the volume knob turns down as well as up.

Remember that as a teenager you are in the last stage of your life when you will be happy to hear the phone is for you. *Fran Lebowitz*

The British have a remarkable talent for keeping calm, even when there is no crisis.

Franklin P. Jones

Some folks can look so busy doing nothing that they seem indispensable. *Kin Hubbard*

Find a job you like and you add five days to every week. *H. Jackson Brown Jr.*